Lerner SPORTS™

ALL-STAR SMACKDOWN

SIDNEY CROSBY VS. WAYNE GRETZKY

WHO WOULD WIN?

JOSH ANDERSON

Lerner Publications ◆ Minneapolis

Lerner Publications Company
An imprint of Lerner Publishing Group, Inc.
241 First Avenue North
Minneapolis, MN 55401 USA

For reading levels and more information, look up this title at www.lernerbooks.com.

Main body text set in Aptifer Sans LT Pro.
Typeface provided by Linotype AG.

Library of Congress Cataloging-in-Publication Data

Names: Anderson, Josh, author.
Title: Sidney Crosby vs. Wayne Gretzky : who would win? / Josh Anderson.
Other titles: Sidney Crosby versus Wayne Gretzky
Description: Minneapolis : Lerner Publications , [2024] | Series: All-star smackdown (lerner sports) | Includes bibliographical references and index. | Audience: Ages 7–11 | Audience: Grades 2–3 | Summary: "NHL legend Wayne Gretzky's nickname was The Great One. When Sidney Crosby joined the NHL in 2005, his nickname was The Next One. So who wins this hockey face-off? Explore their careers to find out"— Provided by publisher.
Identifiers: LCCN 2023017454 (print) | LCCN 2023017455 (ebook) | ISBN 9798765610312 (library binding) | ISBN 9798765623565 (paperback) | ISBN 9798765614143 (epub)
Subjects: LCSH: Crosby, Sidney, 1987—-Juvenile literature. | Gretzky, Wayne, 1961—-Juvenile literature. | Hockey players—Canada—Biography—Juvenile literature. | BISAC: JUVENILE NONFICTION / Sports & Recreation / Hockey | JUVENILE NONFICTION / Biography & Autobiography / Sports & Recreation
Classification: LCC GV848.5.C76 A84 2024 (print) | LCC GV848.5.C76 (ebook) | DDC 796.962092 [B]—dc23/eng/20230421

LC record available at https://lccn.loc.gov/2023017454
LC ebook record available at https://lccn.loc.gov/2023017455

Manufactured in the United States of America
3-1011139-51704-4/29/2024

TABLE OF CONTENTS

Wayne Gretzky

INTRODUCTION

LEGENDS OF THE ICE

After leading the Edmonton Oilers to four Stanley Cup titles in the 1980s, center Wayne Gretzky joined the Los Angeles Kings in 1988. The Kings had never been to the Stanley Cup Finals, the

FAST FACTS

- Wayne Gretzky is the National Hockey League's (NHL) all-time leader in points, goals, and assists.
- Gretzky won the Hart Memorial Trophy nine times as the league's Most Valuable Player (MVP).
- During the 2006-2007 season, Sidney Crosby became the first teenager to lead the NHL in scoring since Gretzky did it in 1980.
- Crosby has led the Penguins to three Stanley Cup championships.

NHL's championship series. But in 1993, Gretzky led the team to the conference finals against the Toronto Maple Leafs. The series winner would go on to play for the Stanley Cup.

The teams were tied after six games. Gretzky was such an amazing player that fans and teammates called him The Great One. He was at his best in Game 7.

With only a few minutes left to play, the Kings held a 4–3 lead. Gretzky had already scored two goals. He skated fast behind Toronto's net. He hoped to sneak the puck in from behind. But Toronto's goalie blocked him.

Gretzky shot the puck toward the front of the goal. The puck bounced off a defender's stick and into the net. Thanks to Gretzky's hat trick, the Kings went to the Stanley Cup Finals for the first time. They lost to the Montreal Canadiens.

Twenty years later, Sidney Crosby led the Pittsburgh Penguins into Game 2 of a 2013 playoff series against the Ottawa Senators. Crosby scored soon after the game started. After Ottawa tied the game, Crosby scored again.

Early in the second period, Crosby received a pass. He lifted his stick high into the air and sent the puck flying past the goalie. He'd achieved a playoff hat trick in just under 22 minutes. The Penguins won the game 4–3. They won the series in five games.

Gretzky and Crosby have each had so many incredible moments in their careers. But which player is the best? Let the smackdown begin!

Sidney Crosby waits for a pass in a 2013 Stanley Cup playoff game against the Boston Bruins.

Crosby had 15 points in 14 games during the 2013 Stanley Cup playoffs.

CHAPTER 1

Wayne Gretzky in his youth team uniform in 1970

JOURNEY TO GREATNESS

Wayne Gretzky was born on January 26, 1961, in Brantford, Ontario, Canada. When Wayne was barely walking, his father built an ice rink in the family's backyard. Wayne was skating before he was three years old.

At the age of six, Wayne played on a hockey team for 10-year-olds. He was younger and smaller than his teammates, but he knew how to score. By the time he was 13, he'd scored more than 1,000 goals for his youth hockey teams.

At the time, the NHL did not allow players under 20. But Wayne was ready to play pro hockey by 17. The World Hockey Association (WHA) tried to compete with the NHL by finding top young players around the world. The WHA did not have a minimum age for players.

Gretzky joined the WHA's Indianapolis Racers in 1978. But the team had money problems and sold him to the

Gretzky practices with the Indianapolis Racers in 1978.

Edmonton Oilers. In the 1978–1979 season, Gretzky scored 104 points and won the WHA's Rookie of the Year award. The next season, the Oilers joined the NHL. The NHL lowered its age rule, allowing Gretzky to play.

Sidney Crosby was born on August 7, 1987, near Halifax, Nova Scotia, Canada. Sidney's father, Troy, was a goalie who played in the Quebec Major Junior Hockey League. Sidney started playing with a hockey stick in his family's basement at the age of two. He learned to skate when he was three.

Crosby was the youngest member of Team Canada at the Under-18 Junior World Cup in 2003.

Crosby competes for his Quebec Major Junior team, Rimouski Océanic, in 2004.

Like Gretzky, Sidney was a skilled youth player. When he was 15, he attended boarding school and played hockey in the US for a year. That season, he led his school to a national championship.

Sidney played two seasons in the Quebec Major Junior Hockey League. He led the league in scoring and won the Player of the Year award both seasons. During that time, he was offered a contract to play in the World Hockey Association, a new league with the same name as the old WHA.

Crosby turned down a $7.5 million contract with the WHA. He was not ready to play pro hockey. And when he was, he wanted it to be in the NHL. In 2005, Sidney entered the NHL Draft. When the Pittsburgh Penguins won the first pick, there was no doubt about who they would choose. Crosby was the pick.

Crosby poses for a photo on draft day in 2005.

CONSIDER THIS

Sidney Crosby chose jersey number 87 based on an important date. He was born on August 7, 1987. That's the eighth month of the year and the seventh day of the month in 1987.

Both Crosby and Gretzky were great players when they were very young. Hockey fans weren't surprised when each of them became NHL legends.

Gretzky takes a slap shot in a 1999 game.

CHAPTER 2

Gretzky during his historic 1981–1982 season

GREAT MOMENTS

Gretzky was one of the NHL's top players from the beginning. In his first season, he tied for the NHL's points lead and won the Hart Memorial Trophy. In his third NHL season, Gretzky's attempt to set a new record was followed closely by fans around the world. No player had ever scored 50 goals in fewer than 50 games.

Coming into the 39th game of the 1981–1982 season, Gretzky had scored 45 goals. He was on pace to break the record. Gretzky scored four goals during the first 55 minutes of the game against the Philadelphia Flyers. This put him at 49 goals for the season. Fans at Northlands Coliseum in Edmonton were hoping to see history. But time was running out.

As the clock ticked down to the game's final seconds, Gretzky took the puck. He skated ahead and shot it toward

Gretzky celebrates his record-breaking 50th goal of the season.

Gretzky (center left) *holds the Stanley Cup in 1988.*

the goal. It zipped into the open net for Gretzky's fifth goal of the game. He'd scored 50 goals in just 39 games, crushing the previous record. He finished the season with 92 goals, the most in NHL history.

Gretzky's scoring total during the 1985–1986 season may never be matched. He set an NHL record with 215 points. Only Mario Lemieux has even come close to matching it. Overall, Gretzky holds nine of the 11 top-scoring seasons in NHL history.

During the 1988 playoffs, Gretzky scored 12 goals and had 31 assists. He won the playoffs MVP award for the second time. Winning his fourth Stanley Cup with the Oilers that

CONSIDER THIS

Gretzky is tied with Brett Hull for the most game-winning goals in NHL playoffs history. Both men finished their careers with 24.

year was his last big win in Edmonton before leaving for Los Angeles, California.

Early in his career, Crosby earned the nickname Sid the Kid for his incredible play. He scored 102 points in 2005–2006, his first NHL season. The next season, he became the

Crosby always plays with his head up, ready for a pass from a teammate.

youngest player ever to lead the NHL in scoring. He was the first teenager to lead the league since Gretzky in 1980.

Crosby helped the Penguins improve. The team reached the 2008 Stanley Cup Finals and lost to the Detroit Red Wings. In 2009, Crosby led the Penguins back to the Finals and a rematch with the Red Wings.

With Detroit leading two games to one, the Penguins needed a victory in Game 4. The teams were tied 2–2 in the second period. Crosby scored the winning goal in a 4–2 victory. After losing the fifth game, the Penguins won the

Crosby and NHL commissioner Gary Bettman hold the Stanley Cup in 2009.

Crosby skates for Team Canada during the 2010 Olympics.

next two games 2–1. They captured the first Stanley Cup of Crosby's career.

One of the biggest goals of Crosby's career came in the gold medal game at the 2010 Olympic Games in Vancouver, Canada. Crosby and Team Canada were playing the United States. The game included some of hockey's biggest stars.

Tied 2–2, the game moved into overtime. Nearly eight minutes into the extra period, Crosby scored to give Canada the victory and the gold medal. Hockey fans in Canada were thrilled. Many consider Crosby's Golden Goal in the Olympics to be the most important of his career.

CHAPTER 3

Gretzky* (right) *and his agent, Mike Barnett* (left), *at the 1987 NHL Awards ceremony

AMAZING STATS

Gretzky and Crosby are two of the most successful hockey players in the history of the sport. Gretzky led his teams to the Stanley Cup Finals six times and won the title four times. Crosby has reached the Finals four times with the Penguins and brought home the Stanley Cup three times.

Gretzky is the all-time NHL leader in points with 2,857. Crosby ranked 15th after the 2022–2023 season with 1,502 points, and he will continue to climb the list. Gretzky holds the NHL record for goals with 894. Crosby ranks 29th with 550. Gretzky is also the NHL's career assists leader with 1,963. Crosby's 952 assists are 16th all-time.

In his career, Gretzky earned nine Hart Memorial Trophies and two Conn Smythe Trophies. Crosby has won both awards twice. Gretzky led the NHL in scoring 11 different times, including eight seasons in a row from 1980 to 1987. Crosby has led the league twice.

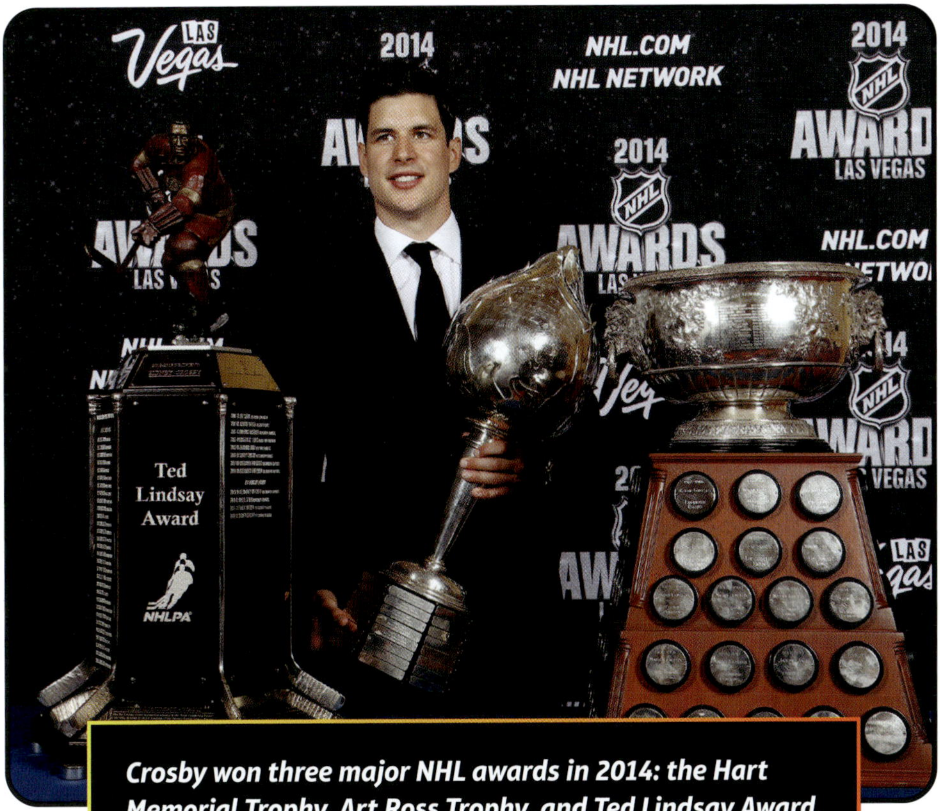

Crosby won three major NHL awards in 2014: the Hart Memorial Trophy, Art Ross Trophy, and Ted Lindsay Award.

CONSIDER THIS

The Penguins have made the playoffs during every season of Sidney Crosby's career except his rookie season in 2005–2006 and 2022–2023.

When the NHL chose its top 100 players of all time in 2017, both Gretzky and Crosby made the list. Gretzky is a member of the Hockey Hall of Fame. Crosby will join the Hall of Fame soon after he retires.

Gretzky* (left) *and Crosby* (second from right) *attend the 2017 NHL Awards with other hockey legends.

Gretzky plays for Canada during the 1998 Winter Olympics.

Gretzky only played for Canada once at the Olympic Games. He competed at the 1998 Olympics in Nagano, Japan. But Team Canada failed to earn a medal. Before that, NHL players did not compete in the Olympics. Crosby represented Canada in the 2010 and 2014 Olympics, leading both teams to gold medals.

CHAPTER 4

Crosby celebrates a Penguins goal.

AND THE WINNER IS

Who is the winner of this smackdown between hockey legends? You can decide for yourself. Wayne Gretzky and Sidney Crosby are among the greatest hockey players of all time, so there is no right or wrong answer. Different people may have different opinions. That's part of the fun of being a sports fan. So who do you think is best? Let's think about their careers.

Both players helped their teams win big games. Gretzky's teams won four Stanley Cups, while Crosby's have won three. Gretzky played 20 seasons in the NHL. Crosby has played fewer, but he would have to play for many more years to come close to Gretzky's stats.

Gretzky sits on the car he earned for winning the 1983 NHL All-Star Game MVP award.

Gretzky's stats are shocking. His 2,857 career points are 936 more than Jaromír Jágr's, who ranks second all-time. That means if Gretzky had never scored a single NHL goal, he'd still be the all-time points leader. He had more assists than any other player's goals and assists combined.

Gretzky's amazing stats and Stanley Cup wins make him the winner of this smackdown. It's usually hard to pick a winner in a contest between two sports legends. But Gretzky's incredible career makes him the clear choice. Who do you think should get the edge? Think it over and make your pick!

The 2022–2023 NHL season marked Crosby's 18th year in the league.

Gretzky takes the ice for the Los Angeles Kings in 1989.

SMACKDOWN BREAKDOWN

WAYNE GRETZKY

Date of birth: January 26, 1961
Height: 6 feet (1.8 m)
Points: 2,857
Goals: 894
Assists: 1,963
Stanley Cup victories: 4

Stats are accurate through the 2022–2023 NHL season.

SIDNEY CROSBY

Date of birth: August 7, 1987
Height: 5 feet 11 (1.8 m)
Points: 1,502
Goals: 550
Assists: 952
Stanley Cup victories: 3

GLOSSARY

assist: a pass that leads to a goal

boarding school: a school where students live during the term

center: a player who usually plays in the middle of the ice

Conn Smythe Trophy: the award given to the MVP of the NHL playoffs

draft: when teams take turns choosing new players

Hart Memorial Trophy: the award given to the NHL's season MVP

hat trick: a three-goal game

Hockey Hall of Fame: a museum in Toronto, Canada, that honors hockey players, coaches, and teams

point: a goal or an assist

rookie: a first-year player

title: a championship

LEARN MORE

Arthur, William. *Pittsburgh Penguins*. Mendota Heights, MN: Press Room Editions, 2022.

Britannica Kids—Ice Hockey
https://kids.britannica.com/kids/article/Ice-Hockey/353257

Doeden, Matt. *G.O.A.T. Hockey Teams*. Minneapolis: Lerner Publications, 2021.

NHL
https://www.nhl.com/

Sports Illustrated Kids—Hockey
https://www.sikids.com/hockey

Walker, Tracy Sue. *Wayne Gretzky: The Great One*. Minneapolis: Lerner Publications, 2023.

INDEX

PHOTO ACKNOWLEDGMENTS

Image credits: ©Mike Powell/Staff/Getty Images, p.4; Bruce Bennett/Contributor/Getty Images, p.5; Brian Babineau/Contributor/Getty Images, p.6; Justin K. Aller/Stringer/Getty Images, p.7; B Bennett/Contributor/Getty Images, p.8; B Bennett/Contributor/Getty Images, p.9; J Kolis/Contributor/Getty Images, p.10; P McCallum/Contributor/Getty Images, p.11; Dave Sandford/Stringer/Getty Images, p.12; B Bennett/Contributor/Getty Images, p.13; Bruce Bennett/Contributor/Getty Images, p.14; Doug Griffin/Contributor/Getty Images, p.15; B Bennett/Contributor/Getty Images, p.16; Icon Sports Wire/Contributor/Getty Images, p.17; Harry How/Staff/Getty Images, p.18; Bruce Bennett/Staff/Getty Images, p.19; B Bennett/Contributor/Getty Images, p.20; Bruce Bennett/Staff/Getty Images, p.21; Jeff Vinnick/Contributor/Getty Images, p.22; B Bennett/Contributor/Getty Images, 23; Emilee Chinn/Stringer/Getty Images, p.24; B Bennett/Contributor/Getty Images, p.25; Justin Berl/Stringer/Getty Images, p.26; Andrew D. Bernstein/Contributor/Getty Images, p.27; B Bennett/Contributor/Getty Images, p.28; Joe Sargent/Contributor/Getty Images, p.29

Cover: ©Bruce Bennett/Getty Images; Josh Lobel/Contributor/Getty Images